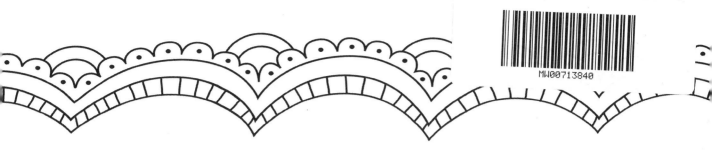

Mommy ♥ Me
Coloring Christmas

Coloring Inspired by Faith

Illustrated By
Jackie Binder

©℗ 2017 Twin Sisters IP, LLC. All Rights Reserved.
Published By Barbour Books, an imprint of Barbour Publishing, Inc.,
P.O. Box 719, Uhrichsville, OH 44683
www.barbourbooks.com

Written By: Kim Mitzo Thompson, Karen Mitzo Hilderbrand
Illustrated By: Jackie Binder
Music By: Hal Wright
Executive Producers: Kim Mitzo Thompson, Karen Mitzo Hilderbrand

This Book Belongs To:

....

....

....

Date

Gloria

IN
EXCELSIS
DEO

Go to www.musicforlearning.com and enter
Promocode: MMCC2017
to download the FREE CHRISTMAS SONGS!

- Silent Night
- The First Noel
- What Child Is This?
- Angels We Have Heard On High
- Joy To The World
- We Three Kings
- Away In A Manger
- Coventry Carol

- Infant So Gentle
- O Holy Night
- I Saw Three Ships
- It Came Upon A Midnight Clear
- Still, Still, Still
- O Come, O Come, Emmanuel
- O Little Town Of Bethlehem
- Hark! The Herald Angels Sing

In the sixth month of Elizabeth's pregnancy, God sent the angel Gabriel to Nazareth, a town in Galilee, to a virgin pledged to be married to a man named Joseph, a descendant of David. The virgin's name was Mary. The angel went to her and said, "Greetings, you who are highly favored! The Lord is with you." Mary was greatly troubled at his words and wondered what kind of greeting this might be. Luke 1:26-29 NIV

_____

_____

_____

_____

☆

_____
Signed

_____
Date

During Elizabeth's sixth month of pregnancy, God sent the angel Gabriel to a virgin who lived in Nazareth, a town in Galilee. She was engaged to marry a man named Joseph from the family of David. Her name was Mary. The angel came to her and said, "Greetings! The Lord has blessed you and is with you." But Mary was very confused by what the angel said. Mary wondered, "What does this mean?" Luke 1:26-29 ICB

_____

Signed

_____

Date

But the angel said to her, "Do not be afraid, Mary; you have found favor with God. You will conceive and give birth to a son, and you are to call him Jesus. He will be great and will be called the Son of the Most High. Luke 1:30-32 NIV

Signed

Date

The angel said to her, "Don't be afraid, Mary, because God is pleased with you. Listen! You will become pregnant. You will give birth to a son, and you will name him Jesus. He will be great, and people will call him the Son of the Most High. Luke 1:30-32 ICB

_____

Signed

_____

Date

But while he thought about these things, behold, an angel of the Lord appeared to him in a dream, saying, "Joseph, son of David, do not be afraid to take to you Mary your wife, for that which is conceived in her is of the Holy Spirit. And she will bring forth a Son, and you shall call His name JESUS, for He will save His people from their sins." So all this was done that it might be fulfilled which was spoken by the Lord through the prophet, saying: "Behold, the virgin shall be with child, and bear a Son, and they shall call His name Immanuel," which is translated, "God with us." Matthew 1:20-23 NKJV

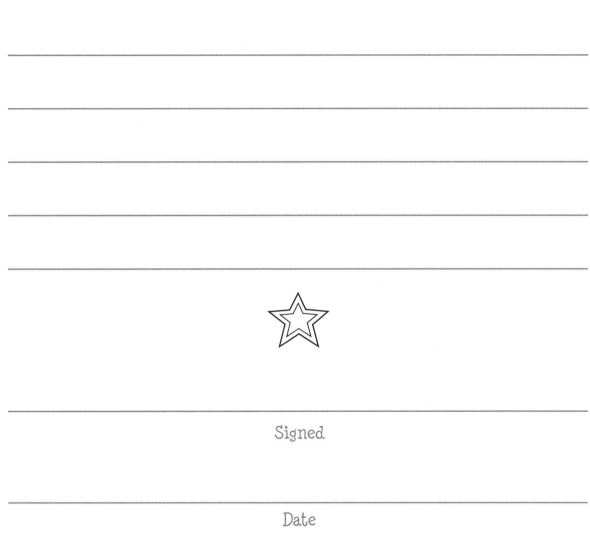

Signed

Date

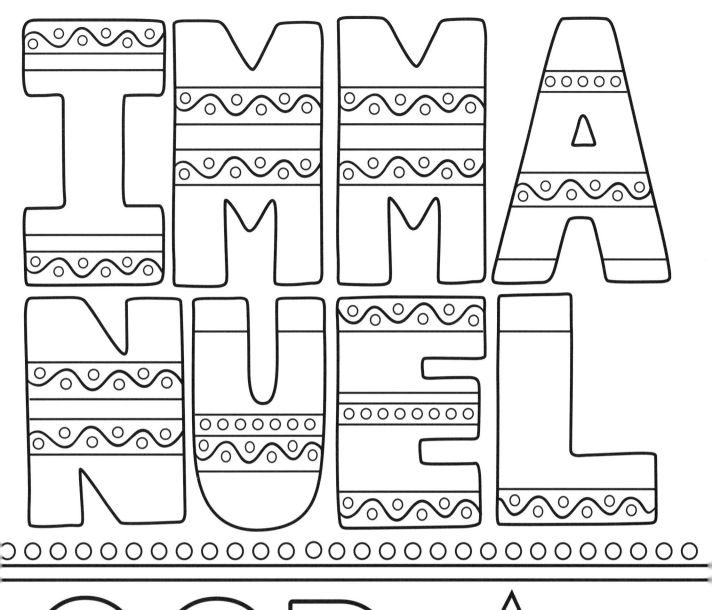

IMMANUEL
GOD ⭐ WITH US

But as Joseph was thinking about this, an angel of the Lord appeared to him in a dream. The angel said, "Joseph, son of David, don't be afraid to take Mary home as your wife. The baby inside her is from the Holy Spirit. She is going to have a son. You must give him the name Jesus. That's because he will save his people from their sins." All this took place to bring about what the Lord had said would happen. He had said through the prophet, "The virgin is going to have a baby. She will give birth to a son. And he will be called Immanuel." (Isaiah 7:14) The name Immanuel means "God with us." Matthew 1:20-23 NIRV

_____

Signed

_____

Date

And Mary said:

"My soul glorifies the Lord and my spirit rejoices in God my Savior,
for he has been mindful of the humble state of his servant.
From now on all generations will call me blessed, for the Mighty One
has done great things for me—holy is his name." Luke 1:46-49 NIV

_____

_____

_____

_____

_____

☆

_____

Signed

_____

Date

Then Mary said,

"My soul praises the Lord; my heart is happy because God is my Savior. I am not important, but God has shown his care for me, his servant girl. From now on, all people will say that I am blessed, because the Powerful One has done great things for me. His name is holy." Luke 1:46-49 ICB

_____

Signed

_____

Date

In those days Caesar Augustus issued a decree that a census should be taken of the entire Roman world. (This was the first census that took place while Quirinius was governor of Syria.) And everyone went to their own town to register. So Joseph also went up from the town of Nazareth in Galilee to Judea, to Bethlehem the town of David, because he belonged to the house and line of David. He went there to register with Mary, who was pledged to be married to him and was expecting a child. Luke 2:1-5 NIV

_____

_____

_____

_____

☆

_____

Signed

_____

Date

In those days, Caesar Augustus made a law. It required that a list be made of everyone in the whole Roman world. It was the first time a list was made of the people while Quirinius was governor of Syria. Everyone went to their own town to be listed. So Joseph went also. He went from the town of Nazareth in Galilee to Judea. That is where Bethlehem, the town of David, was. Joseph went there because he belonged to the family line of David. He went there with Mary to be listed. Mary was engaged to him. She was expecting a baby.
Luke 2:1-5 NIRV

_____

Signed

_____

Date

And so it was, that, while they were there, the days were accomplished that she should be delivered. And she brought forth her firstborn son, and wrapped him in swaddling clothes, and laid him in a manger; because there was no room for them in the inn. Luke 2:6-7 KJV

_____

_____

_____

_____

☆

_____

Signed

_____

Date

While they were there, the time came for the baby to be born, and she gave birth to her firstborn, a son. She wrapped him in cloths and placed him in a manger, because there was no guest room available for them. Luke 2:6-7 NIV

_____

Signed

_____

Date

And there were shepherds living out in the fields nearby, keeping watch over their flocks at night. An angel of the Lord appeared to them, and the glory of the Lord shone around them, and they were terrified. But the angel said to them, "Do not be afraid. I bring you good news that will cause great joy for all the people. Today in the town of David a Savior has been born to you; he is the Messiah, the Lord. This will be a sign to you: You will find a baby wrapped in cloths and lying in a manger." Luke 2:8-12 NIV

☆

_____
Signed

_____
Date

GOOD NEWS of GREAT JOY

That night, some shepherds were in the fields nearby watching their sheep. An angel of the Lord stood before them. The glory of the Lord was shining around them, and suddenly they became very frightened. The angel said to them, "Don't be afraid, because I am bringing you some good news. It will be a joy to all the people. Today your Savior was born in David's town. He is Christ, the Lord. This is how you will know him: You will find a baby wrapped in cloths and lying in a feeding box." Luke 2:8-12 ICB

_____

Signed

_____

Date

Suddenly a great company of the heavenly host appeared with the angel, praising God and saying, "Glory to God in the highest heaven, and on earth peace to those on whom his favor rests." Luke 2:13-14 NIV

_____

_____

_____

_____

☆

_____

Signed

_____

Date

Then a very large group of angels from heaven joined the first angel.
All the angels were praising God, saying: "Give glory to God in heaven,
and on earth let there be peace to the people who please God."
Luke 2:13-14 ICB

_____

Signed

_____

Date

When the angels had left them and gone into heaven, the shepherds said to one another, "Let's go to Bethlehem and see this thing that has happened, which the Lord has told us about." So they hurried off and found Mary and Joseph, and the baby, who was lying in the manger. When they had seen him, they spread the word concerning what had been told them about this child, and all who heard it were amazed at what the shepherds said to them. But Mary treasured up all these things and pondered them in her heart. The shepherds returned, glorifying and praising God for all the things they had heard and seen, which were just as they had been told. Luke 2:15-20 NIV

_____

_____

_____

_____

_____

_____

Signed

_____

Date

Then the angels left the shepherds and went back to heaven. The shepherds said to each other, "Let us go to Bethlehem and see this thing that has happened. We will see this thing the Lord told us about." So the shepherds went quickly and found Mary and Joseph. And the shepherds saw the baby lying in a feeding box. Then they told what the angels had said about this child. Everyone was amazed when they heard what the shepherds said to them. Mary hid these things in her heart; she continued to think about them. Then the shepherds went back to their sheep, praising God and thanking him for everything that they had seen and heard. It was just as the angel had told them. Luke 2:15-20 ICB

_____

Signed

_____

Date

When they heard the king, they departed; and behold, the star which they had seen in the East went before them, till it came and stood over where the young Child was. When they saw the star, they rejoiced with exceedingly great joy. Matthew 2:9-10 NKJV

_____

_____

_____

_____

☆

_____
Signed

_____
Date

When they saw the star,
they rejoiced with exceedingly
great joy.

After the Wise Men had listened to the king, they went on their way.
The star they had seen when it rose went ahead of them. It finally
stopped over the place where the child was. When they saw the star,
they were filled with joy. Matthew 2:9-10 NIRV

_____

Signed

_____

Date

And when they had come into the house, they saw the young Child with Mary His mother, and fell down and worshiped Him. And when they had opened their treasures, they presented gifts to Him: gold, frankincense, and myrrh. Matthew 2:11 NKJV

_____

_____

_____

_____

☆

_____
Signed

_____
Date

The Wise Men went to the house. There they saw the child with his mother Mary. They bowed down and worshiped him. Then they opened their treasures. They gave him gold, frankincense and myrrh.
Matthew 2:11 NIRV

_____

Signed

_____

Date

For unto us a Child is born,
Unto us a Son is given;
And the government will be upon His shoulder.
And His name will be called Wonderful, Counselor, Mighty God,
Everlasting Father, Prince of Peace. Isaiah 9:6 NKJV

_____

_____

_____

_____

_____

_____

Signed

_____

Date

And he will be called Wonderful Counselor, Mighty God, Everlasting Father, Prince of Peace. Isaiah 9:6 NIV

_____

Signed

_____

Date

For God so loved the world that he gave his one and only Son, that whoever believes in him shall not perish but have eternal life. For God did not send his Son into the world to condemn the world, but to save the world through him. John 3:16-17 NIV

_____

_____

_____

_____

☆

_____

Signed

_____

Date

For God So Loved
The World

God so loved the world that he gave his one and only Son. Anyone who believes in him will not die but will have eternal life. God did not send his Son into the world to judge the world. He sent his Son to save the world through him. John 3:16-17 NIRV

_____

Signed

_____

Date

Joy to the world, the Savior reigns!
Let men their songs employ;
While fields and floods, rocks, hills and plains
Repeat the sounding joy,
Repeat the sounding joy,
Repeat, repeat the sounding joy.

He rules the world with truth and grace,
And makes the nations prove
The glories of His righteousness,
And wonders of His love,
And wonders of His love,
And wonders, wonders, of His love.

_____

Signed

_____

Date

Joy to the world, the Lord is come!
Let earth receive her King;
Let every heart prepare Him room,
And heaven and nature sing,
And heaven and nature sing,
And heaven, and heaven, and nature sing.

_____

Signed

_____

Date

Shepherds, why this jubilee?
Why your joyous strains prolong?
What the gladsome tidings be
Which inspire your heavenly song?
Gloria, in excelsis Deo!
Gloria, in excelsis Deo!

Come to Bethlehem and see
Christ whose birth the angels sing;
Come, adore on bended knee,
Christ the Lord, the newborn King!
Gloria, in excelsis Deo!
Gloria, in excelsis Deo!

_____

Signed

_____

Date

Angels we have heard on high
Sweetly singing o'er the plains,
And the mountains in reply
Echoing their joyous strains.
Gloria, in excelsis Deo!
Gloria, in excelsis Deo!

Signed

Date

They looked up and saw a star
Shining in the east, beyond them far;
And to the earth it gave great light,
And so it continued both day and night.
Noel, Noel, Noel, Noel,
Born is the King of Israel.

And by the light of that same star
Three wise men came from country far;
To seek for a King was their intent,
And to follow the star wherever it went.
Noel, Noel, Noel, Noel,
Born is the King of Israel.

_____

Signed

_____

Date

The first Noel the angels did say
Was to certain poor shepherds in fields as they lay;
In fields where they lay keeping their sheep,
On a cold winter's night that was so deep.
Noel, Noel, Noel, Noel,
Born is the King of Israel.

_____

Signed

_____

Date

Silent night, holy night.
Son of God, love's pure light;
Radiant beams from Thy holy face
With the dawn of redeeming grace,
Jesus, Lord, at Thy birth,
Jesus, Lord, at Thy birth.

_____

Signed

_____

Date

Silent night, holy night,
All is calm, all is bright
Round yon virgin mother and Child.
Holy Infant, so tender and mild,
Sleep in heavenly peace,
Sleep in heavenly peace.

_____

Signed

_____

Date

Away in a manger, no crib for a bed,
The little Lord Jesus laid down His sweet head.
The stars in the sky looked down where He lay,
The little Lord Jesus, asleep on the hay.

_____

Signed

_____

Date

Be near me, Lord Jesus, I ask Thee to stay
Close by me forever, and love me, I pray;
Bless all the dear children in Thy tender care,
And take us to heaven to live with Thee there.

_____

Signed

_____

Date

How silently, how silently,
The wondrous Gift is giv'n;
So God imparts to human hearts
The blessings of His heav'n.
No ear may hear His coming,
But in this world of sin,
Where meek souls will receive Him still,
The dear Christ enters in.

_____

Signed

_____

Date

O little town of Bethlehem,
How still we see thee lie!
Above thy deep and dreamless sleep
The silent stars go by.
Yet in thy dark streets shineth
The everlasting Light;
The hopes and fears of all the years
Are met in thee tonight.

Signed

Date

O come, Thou Day-spring, come and cheer
Our spirits by Thine advent here;
Disperse the gloomy clouds of night,
And death's dark shadows put to flight.
Rejoice! Rejoice!
Emmanuel shall come to thee, O Israel.

O come, Thou Key of David, come,
And open wide our heavenly home;
Make safe the way that leads on high
And close the path to misery.
Rejoice! Rejoice!
Emmanuel shall come to thee, O Israel.

_____

Signed

_____

Date

REJOICE! REJOICE!

O come, O come, Emmanuel,
And ransom captive Israel,
That mourns in lonely exile here
Until the Son of God appear.
Rejoice! Rejoice!
Emmanuel shall come to thee, O Israel.

_____

Signed

_____

Date

So bring Him incense, gold, and myrrh,
Come peasant, king to own Him;
The King of kings salvation brings,
Let loving hearts enthrone Him.
Raise, raise a song on high,
The virgin sings her lullaby.
Joy, joy for Christ is born,
The Babe, the Son of Mary.

_____

Signed

_____

Date

Whom angels greet with
**ANTHEMS
SWEET**

What Child is this who, laid to rest
On Mary's lap is sleeping?
Whom angels greet with anthems sweet,
While shepherds watch are keeping?
This, this is Christ the King,
Whom shepherds guard and angels sing;
Haste, haste, to bring Him laud,
The Babe, the Son of Mary.

_____

Signed

_____

Date

Born a King on Bethlehem's plain
Gold I bring to crown Him again,
King forever, ceasing never,
Over us all to reign.
O star of wonder, star of light,
Star with royal beauty bright,
Westward leading, still proceeding,
Guide us to thy perfect light.

Glorious now behold Him arise;
King and God and sacrifice;
Alleluia, Alleluia,
Earth to the heavens replies.
O star of wonder, star of light,
Star with royal beauty bright,
Westward leading, still proceeding,
Guide us to thy perfect light.
Guide us to thy perfect light.

_____

Signed

_____

Date

We three kings of Orient are;
Bearing gifts we traverse afar,
Field and fountain, moor and mountain,
Following yonder star.
O star of wonder, star of light,
Star with royal beauty bright,
Westward leading, still proceeding,
Guide us to thy perfect light.

Signed

Date

Hail the heav'n-born Prince of Peace,
Hail, the Sun of Righteousness!
Light and life to all He brings,
Ris'n with healing in His wings.
Mild He lays His glory by,
Born that man no more may die.
Born to raise the sons of earth,
Born to give them second birth.
Hark! The herald angels sing,
"Glory to the newborn King."

_____

Signed

_____

Date

Hark! The herald angels sing, "Glory to the newborn King;
Peace on earth, and mercy mild, God and sinners reconciled!"
Joyful, all ye nations, rise. Join the triumph of the skies.
With th' angelic host proclaim, "Christ is born in Bethlehem!"
Hark! The herald angels sing, "Glory to the newborn King."

_____

Signed

_____

Date